The Estonian Christmas Cookbook

Lucie Rogers

Contents

Introduction

Christmas is a popular time in Estonia. The Estonian Christmas has many familiar traditions from western and northern European festive celebrations. Estonia's Nordic, wintry climate also helps to create a Christmas atmosphere. Estonian cultural, rural and pagan traditions have also influenced the Estonian Christmas and create some unique Christmas customs.

Food is naturally a big part of Christmas. Estonia's traditional foods include rye bread, pork, cabbage, potatoes and dairy products and these play a big part in Estonia's Christmas meals. Estonians enjoy fresh seasonal ingredients and these help create a variety of Christmas dishes. Of course, a wide range of indulgent festive foods such as cookies, cakes and chocolate dishes are also enjoyed.

Try some Estonian Christmas food with this book - The Estonian Christmas Cookbook.

Mushroom and Barley Soup

Ingredients

30g/1 oz of dried mushrooms
180g/7 oz of barley
2 chopped carrots
2 chopped potatoes
80g/3 oz of chopped green beans
8 cups of beef stock/broth
230g/8 oz of butter
salt
pepper
parsley
sour cream

Put the mushrooms in 240ml/1 cup of warm water. Leave for 40 minutes. Drain and keep the liquid. Chop the mushrooms.

Put 500ml/2 cups of water in a pan. Bring to the boil. Add the barley, cover and cook on a low heat for 17 minutes. Add the butter.

Mix the mushroom water with the beef stock. Put in a pot with the carrots, potatoes, green beans, some parsley and some salt and pepper. Cook on a low heat for 7 minutes. Add the barley. Stir, cover, then cook on a low heat for 1 hour. Add some salt and pepper.

Add some sour cream to the soup portions.

Cheese Dumplings

Ingredients

200g/7 oz of cream cheese
3 eggs
430g/15 oz of flour
85g/3 oz of butter
salt

Mix the egg, cheese, butter, half the flour and some salt.

Rub the mix through a sieve. Add the rest of the flour to the mix. Form into balls. Place in boiling water for 20 minutes; they are ready when they float to the top.

Fried Mushrooms in Sour Cream

Ingredients

400g/14 oz of sliced mushrooms
2 tablespoons of of dried breadcrumbs
120ml/half a cup of sour cream
4 tablespoons of butter
half a finely chopped onion

Cook the onions in the butter for 6 minutes. Add the mushrooms and cook for 5 minutes. Add the breadcrumbs and mix. Remove from the heat.

Whisk the sour cream in a bowl for 3 minutes. Add to the Mushroom mix.

Potato Pancake

Ingredients

226g/8 oz of chopped bacon
5 grated potatoes
120g/1 cup of flour
1 grated/minced onion
2 grated carrots
salt
pepper

Put the bacon in a pan and cook for 8 minutes.

Put the potato, carrot and onion in a bowl and mix. Add the bacon. add the flour and some salt and pepper and mix.

Put some parchment paper on a baking tray. Spread over the potato mix.

Cook in a preheated oven at 200C/400F for 1 hour and 10 minutes.

Potato and Bacon Porridge

Ingredients

600g/1.3 lb of potatoes cut in half
120g/4.2 oz of barley
120g/4.2 oz of chopped bacon
1 chopped onion
2 chopped carrots
210ml/7 fl oz of buttermilk
2 tablespoons of chopped dill
2 tablespoons of chopped spring onion
2 tablespoons of chopped peppermint

Mix the buttermilk and chopped herbs. Put in the refrigerator.

Put the carrot, potato and barley in a pan. Cover with water. Add some salt and pepper. Bring to the boil, then cook for 15 minutes on a low heat - until the vegetables and barley are cooked.

Fry the bacon and onion for 10 minutes in a pan.

Mash the vegetables and barley in the pan. Add the onion and bacon. Serve with the buttermilk and herb sauce.

Liver Pate

Ingredients

500g/1.1 lb of chopped calves liver
160g/6 oz of sliced bacon
2 chopped carrots
2 chopped onions
110g/4 oz of butter
1 tablespoon of brandy
nutmeg
sugar
pepper

Put the onion, carrot and bacon in a pan and cook for 6 minutes. Add the liver and cook for 6 minutes.

Add 150ml/half a pint of water along with the nutmeg, brandy, sugar and some pepper. Blend to make a smooth mix. Blend in the butter.

Put in a dish and refrigerate for 4 hours.

Cheese Soup

Ingredients

300g/10 oz of grated cheese
1 egg yolk
230ml/1 cup of sour cream
1.2 litres/5 cups of water
3 tablespoons of flour
1 teaspoon of salt
half a teaspoon of pepper
white croutons
55g/2 oz of butter

Melt the butter in a pan. Add the flour and mix to make a paste. Add the water, pepper and salt. Bring to the boil. Lower the heat. Mix the sour cream with the yolk. Add to the soup stirring all the time.

Put some cheese in a bowl. Pour over the soup. Top with croutons.

Beetroot and Milk Soup

Ingredients

1.2 litres/5 cups of sour milk
230g/8 oz or cucumber
3 boiled and chopped potatoes
3 chopped boiled eggs
2 boiled and chopped beetroots
100g/3.5 oz of chopped dill
50g/1.7 oz of chopped parsley
2 chopped garlic cloves
50g/1.7 oz of chopped spring or green onion
1 teaspoon of salt
1 teaspoon of pepper

To make the sour milk mix 1.2 litres/5 cups of milk with 5 tablespoons of lemon juice. Leave for 5 minutes.

Put the ingredients in a bowl. Stir gently. Serve chilled.

Rutabaga Mash

Ingredients

800g/1.7 lb of peeled and chopped turnip/rutabaga
50g/1.7 oz of farina
1 teaspoon of salt
half a teaspoon of sugar
half a teaspoon of nutmeg
60ml/1 quarter of a cup of milk
50g/1.7 oz of butter

Put the farina and milk in a pan. Mix and bring to the boil, then cook on a low heat for 10 minutes.

Put 500ml/2 cups of water in a pan. Bring to the boil. Add the turnip and cook on a low heat for 15 minutes - until soft.

Drain. Put in a bowl and mash. Add the farina (while it is hot), salt, sugar, nutmeg and butter and mix well.

Red Cabbage with Apple

Ingredients

1 red cabbage
2 sliced onions
2 peeled, cored and sliced green apples
2 tablespoons of brown sugar
3 cloves
3 allspice berries
110ml/half a cup of apple juice
40ml/1.3 fl oz or red wine vinegar
1 teaspoon of salt
1 teaspoon of pepper
butter

Cook the onions in some butter on a low heat for 17
minutes. Add the sugar, vinegar, cloves, allspice berries
and some salt and pepper. Stir, then add the cabbage.
Cook on a medium heat for 8 minutes. Cover and cook on
a low heat for 17 minutes, stirring several times.

Add the apple juice and apple slices. Cook on a low heat
for 8 minutes.

Estonian Christmas Facts

Christmas in Estonia starts on first advent - the fourth Sunday before December 25th. People buy Advent calendars and light Advent candles.

The main Christmas day in Estonia is Christmas Eve - December 24th.

Christmas is called jõulud in Estonian.

In Estonia Santa Claus brings gifts to children on 24th December.

The home Christmas tree in Estonia was adopted from Germany in the 19th Century.

Germans in Estonia started having a Christmas tree in the house and the tradition caught on with the rest of the population.

Christmas was not officially celebrated when Estonia was occupied by the Soviet Union between 1940-91.

The only holiday was New Year's Eve and New Year's Day.

Christmas Day was a normal workday.

Barley Salad

Ingredients

150g/5.3 oz of barley
550ml/1 pint of water
ham slices
grated cheese
chopped lettuce
grated carrot
grated apple
chopped spring or green onions
fresh thyme
sour cream
salt
pepper

Put the barley in a pan with the water. Add some salt.
Boil, then cover and cook for 25 minutes on a low heat.
Drain.

Mix some sour cream with some salt and pepper.

Put some barley on an individual serving plate. Add some
grated cheese, chopped lettuce, sliced ham, grated carrot,
grated apple, chopped onion and thyme stems. Put some
spoonfuls sour cream on the salad.

Apple and Lingonberry Salad

Ingredients

320g/11 oz of chopped lingonberries
320g/11 oz of grated apples
120ml/4 fl oz of sour cream

Mix the ingredients. Serve with poultry or game.

Beetroot and Milk Soup

Cheese Soup

Sauerkraut with Pork and Barley

Pork in Jelly

Cucumber Salad

Ingredients

400g/14 oz of sliced cucumber
2 teaspoons of salt
2 tablespoons of chopped dill
2 tablespoons of chopped chives

Put the ingredients in a plastic container. Put the lid on.
Gently shake the container for 1 minute.

Herb Mayonnaise

Ingredients

300g/10 oz of mayonnaise
50g/1.7 oz of chopped herbs such as green onion, wild garlic and chives

Blend the ingredients to make a smooth mix.

Beetroot and Potato Salad

Ingredients

1 medium salted herring with bones and skin removed
300g/10 oz of beetroot
580g/1.2 lb of potatoes
150g/5 oz of carrots
2 dill pickles
2 cored, peeled and chopped apples
4 hard boiled eggs
100ml/3.3 fl oz of sour cream
half a teaspoon of mustard
1 teaspoon of sugar
salt

Steam the vegetables whole and unpeeled until cooked. Steam the beetroot for 30 minutes. Steam potatoes for 15 minutes. Steam carrots for 5 minutes.

Peel the vegetables and chop them up. Chop up the fish.

Mix he sour cream, sugar, salt and mustard. Put the vegetables, pickles, fish and apples in a bowl. Add the sour cream mix and stir. Place in the refrigerator for 2 hours.

Cover with chopped egg before serving.

Pickled Pumpkin

Ingredients

1.3 kg/3 lb of peeled and chopped pumpkin
800g/4 cups of sugar
12 cloves
3 sticks of cinnamon
1 litre/4 cups of white vinegar

Put the vinegar, sugar, cloves and cinnamon in a pan.
Bring to the boil then cook for 6 minutes. Put the
pumpkin in a bowl. Pour over the liquid. Cover and leave
for 9 hours.

Strain the liquid. Put in a saucepan. Take out the
cinnamon and cloves. Boil the liquid for 6 minutes. Add
the pumpkin and boil for another 6 minutes.

Leave to cool, then put into jars and store in the
refrigerator.

Sprat and Rye Bread Sandwich

Kiluvoileib

Ingredients

dark rye bread slices
butter
sprat fillets
finely diced red onion
gherkin slices
boiled egg slices
munavoi (chopped boiled eggs and butter mixed together)
chopped green onions
dill

Butter the bread. Some munovi can be added. Add sprat fillets. Top with a selection of boiled egg slices, gherkin slices, green onion and dill.

Munavoi

Ingredients

4 chopped hard boiled eggs
3 tablespoons of butter
salt

Mix the eggs and butter together. Add some salt. Can be served on toast or in sandwiches.

Pea and Smoked Pork Soup

Hernesupp Suitsukoodiga

Ingredients

700g/1 and a half lb of smoked pork hock
200g/7 oz of barley
1 onion cut in half
1 carrot cut in half
2 grated carrots
280g/10 oz of dried peas
2 chopped onions
1 bay leaf
5 peppercorns
salt
pepper
chopped chives

Put the barley and peas in some cold water in a bowl.
Leave for 24 hours.

Put the pork on hock in a pan. Cover with water. Bring to
the boil. Add the halved onion, halved carrot,
peppercorns, bay leaf and some salt and pepper. Cook on
a low heat for 2 hours.

Strain the liquid.

Remove the meat from the bone and cut it up.

Drain the barley and peas. Add to the pan with the
strained liquid. Fry the grated carrot and chopped onion

in some oil for 7 minutes. Add to the pan. cook for 1 and a half hours. Add some salt and pepper.

Serve with pieces of meat and some chives.

Smoked Herring Dip

Ingredients

226g/8 oz of chopped smoked herring
1 tablespoon of lemon juice
220ml/8 fl oz of sour cream
chopped dill
1 tablespoon of chopped red onion
salt
pepper

Mix the ingredients.

Estonian Christmas Facts

On the 24th December the President of Estonia declares Christmas. This tradition began in Estonia over 350 years ago after an order by Queen Kristina of Sweden.

On the first day of Advent children in Estonia put their socks in a window ledge. Every day until Christmas Eve an elf visits and puts sweets in the socks.

Tangerines and mandarins are a traditional Estonian Christmas food. These and apples and gingerbread are often served to guests over Christmas.

In Estonian, Merry Christmas is häid jõule.

In Estonian, Santa Claus is called Jõuluvana - Old Yule.

It is said of the Estonian Christmas that it is a mixture of old Estonian folk, pagan traditions and familiar western European Christmas traditions.

An Estonian Christmas tradition is to have a sauna on Christmas Eve.

The Estonian Christmas tree is traditionally decorated on December 21st - on the Feast of St. Thomas. It remains up until January 6th the Feast of Three Kings.

Potato Salad

Ingredients

4 chopped boiled potatoes
2 chopped boiled potatoes
1 grated boiled egg
110g/3.8 oz of chopped smoked sausage
1 chopped apple
half a chopped cucumber
90g/3.1 oz of tinned peas
180g/6.3 oz or mayonnaise
180g/6.3 oz of sour cream
salt
pepper

To boil the carrots, place in boiling water and boil for 5 minutes. To boil the potatoes, place in a pan of boiling water then cook on a medium heat for 10 minutes.

Mix the sour cream and mayonnaise. Add some salt and pepper.

Put the rest of the ingredients in a bowl. Add the sour cream mix.

Salmon with Cranberry

Ingredients

1 salmon fillet
56g/2 oz of chopped dill
150ml/5 fl oz of cranberry juice
1 tablespoon of crushed peppercorns
141g/5 oz of sea salt
200g/7 oz of sugar

Mix the salt, sugar, dill, peppercorns and cranberry juice. Put some of the mix on the bottom of a dish. Put the fish on the dish, skin side down. Put the rest of the mix on top. cover the dish with clingfilm/plastic wrap. Put in the refrigerator and leave for 2 days. Put more mix on the salmon using spoon at least 10 times during the 2 days.

Rinse the salmon in cold water. Dry suing a paper towel. Wrap the salmon in clingfilm/plastic wrap and store in the refrigerator. It can be kept up to 1 week.

Fish Cakes

Ingredients

240g/8.4 oz of chopped salmon
240g/8.4 oz of chopped cod
1 egg
2 tablespoons of lemon juice
2 tablespoons of chopped fresh dill
2 tablespoons of capers
salt
butter
oil

Mix the fish, egg, dill, lemon juice, capers and some salt.

Heat some butter with the same amount of oil in a pan. Form the mix into patties and fry on a medium heat for 5 minutes on each side.

Fried Herring

Ingredients

4 herring fillets
2 tablespoons of rye flour
butter
salt
pepper

Season the fish with some salt and pepper. Coat them in rye flour.

Heat some butter in a pan. Fry the fish on both sides until golden brown.

Roast Goose with Apple

Ingredients

1 goose
8 sliced apples
3 teaspoons of cinnamon
half a teaspoon of allspice
salt
pepper
5 tablespoons of brandy
oil

Prick the skin of the goose with a fork. Mix the allspice and half a teaspoon of cinnamon together. Rub the mix on the goose.

Fry the apples in some oil in a pan for 8 minutes. Add the brandy and mix.

Stuff the goose with the apple mix. Wrap the goose in tin foil (leave a hole) and place on a baking dish. Cook in a preheated oven at 200C/392F for 15 minutes for 450g/1 lb of weight of goose. Add another 25 minutes at the end of cooking. Baste regularly during cooking.

Leave the goose for 20 minutes to rest before carving. Serve with the stuffing.

Chicken and Juniper

Ingredients

6 chicken breast fillets
16 chopped juniper berries
1 tablespoon of fresh chopped dill
1 teaspoon of cornflour/cornstarch
oil
210ml/7 fl oz of sour cream
210ml/7 fl oz of warm chicken stock

Put the chicken on a baking dish. Add the juniper and dill.
Add some salt and pepper and some oil. Cook in a
preheated oven at 160C/320F for 20 minutes.

Mix the cornflour and sour cream. Stir in the stock. Pour
over the chicken. Cook for another 20 minutes - until
chicken is cooked.

Pork Chops in Cream

Ingredients

6 pork chops (with no bone)
230g/8 oz of sliced mushrooms
3 tablespoons of butter
120ml/half a cup of cream
salt
pepper
150ml/5 fl oz of chicken stock

Cook the pork chops in the butter for 3 minutes on each side. Add the stock and cook for 6 minutes.

Take the pork out the pan. Put the cream and mushrooms in the pan. Cook on medium heat for 7 minutes, stirring all the time, until the sauce has thickened. Add the chops and cook on a low heat for 4 minutes.

Sauerkraut with Pork and Barley

Mugikapsas

Ingredients

1920g/2 lb of sauerkraut
430g/15 oz of chopped bacon
4 (350g/12 oz) smoked bacon ribs
100g/half a cup of pearl barley
2 chopped onions
1 teaspoon of honey
salt
1 bay leaf
oil

Put the sauerkraut and barley in a pan with the ribs, bay leaf and bacon. Cover with water. Cook on a low heat for 3 hours - until the meat and barley are cooked. Add some salt and the honey.

Take the bay leaf out and discard. Take the rib meat off the bones and put back in the pan.

Fry the onions in some oil for 8 minutes. Add to the sauerkraut.

Pork in Jelly

Sült

Ingredients

2 legs of pork with the feet attached
400g/14 oz of beef
2 sliced carrots
3 onions
1 garlic clove
10 peppercorns
2 bay leaves
salt

Put the meat in a pan. Cover with water. Bring to the boil, then cook on a low heat for 1 hour.

Add the garlic, carrots and onion. Cook on a low heat for 4 hours.

Add the salt, bay leaf and peppercorns. Boil for 20 minutes.

Take the meat out and take the meat off the bones. Chop the meat.

Put the meat back in the pan. Bring to the boil. Pour the liquid into a bowl and leave to firm up. Can also be poured into glass jars to store if not wanted immediately.

Estonian Christmas Facts

Tallinn Christmas Market is held every year. It is held in the old Town Hall Square. From the last week in November until the first week in January. There are handicrafts, souvenirs as well as Christmas food and drink. It normally attracts around 200,000 visitors each year.

It is said that Tallinn, the Estonian capital, had the first ever Christmas tree put on display in Europe. A tree was erected in the Town Hall Square by the business guild the Brotherhood of Blackheads in 1441.

A key dish in the Estonian Christmas Eve dinner is the blood sausage. They are mostly bought now rather than homemade.

The Estonian Headquarters of Santa Claus is based in Jõgeva, a town in the centre of Estonia. There is a shop there which can be visited. Letters to the post office at Santa Claus Post Office in Jõgeva will be answered.

Piparkoogid - gingerbread biscuits - and marzipan are popular sweets in Estonian at Christmas.

Spiced mulled wine - glögi - is a popular Christmas drink. It can be alcoholic and non alcoholic, and homemade or shop bought.

Steak in Cream Sauce

Ingredients

900g/2 lb steak slices
4 sliced onions
3 tablespoons of flour
70ml/2.3 fl oz sour cream
500ml/2 cups of beef stock/broth
butter
oil
salt
pepper

Add some salt and pepper to the steak. Put an equal amount of butter and oil in a pan and fry the steak on a medium heat until brown on both sides. Put the meat on a plate.

Put the flour in the pan with one tablespoonful of butter. Cook for 2 minutes stirring to make a paste. Add the stock and stir to make a sauce. Put the meat back in the pan and cook on a low heat for 15 minutes -until the beef is cooked.

Put the meat on a plate. Put the sour cream in the pan and cook for 4 minutes. Add some salt and pepper.

In another pan, fry the onion in an equal amount of butter and oil for 15 minutes until crispy.

Serve the beef covered in sauce and topped with onions.

Chicken Schnitzel

Ingredients

chicken fillets
beaten egg
rye bread crumbs
salt
pepper
oil
finely chopped parsley

Beat the chicken fillets with a meat hammer to make them a bit flatter.

Put beaten egg and flour in separate bowls.

Add some salt and pepper to the egg and flour. Add parsley to the flour.

Dip the chicken in the egg and then the breadcrumbs.

Fry in hot oil on both sides until golden brown.

Red Cabbage with Apple

Semla

Gingerbread

Mulled Wine

Roast Pork and Sauerkraut

Ingredients

1 pork joint (e.g. belly)
700g/1 and a half lb of sauerkraut
1 grated carrot
300ml/10 fl oz of stock
100ml/3.4 fl oz of water
100ml/3.4 fl oz of dark beer
2 teaspoons of honey
salt
pepper
oil

Add some salt and pepper to the pork. Cut some sluices in the skin of the pork. Put in a baking dish with a little oil and place in a preheated oven at 148C/300°F for 4 minutes on each side.

Add 240ml/1 cup of hot water to the dish. Cook at 200C/2392F for 1 and a half hours (1 and a half hours per kg).

Leave the pork for 20 minutes before cutting into slices.

For the sauerkraut, put the sauerkraut, grated carrot, stock, water and beer in a pan. Cook on a low heat for 1 and a half hours.

Bread Soup

Ingredients

7 chopped rye bread slices
90g/3.1 oz of raisins
2 peeled and chopped apples
3 prunes - with stone removed
85g/3 oz of fresh cranberries
110g/4 oz of sugar
4 tablespoons of lemon juice
1 teaspoon of cinnamon
1 teaspoon of lemon zest
2 cloves

Put the sugar in a pan with 5 cups of water. Bring to the boil and boil for 5 minutes.

Add the bread then cook on a low heat for 6 minutes.

Remove the bread from the pan and push it through a sieve, or blend gently in a food processor.

Put the bread back into the pan. Add the apples, prunes, cranberries, raisins, lemon juice, lemon zest, cinnamon and cloves. Bring to the boil then cook on a low heat for 12 minutes - until the apples are cooked.

Remove the cloves, the refrigerate the soup for 1 hour before serving.

Rye Biscuits

Ingredients

6 tablespoons of butter
110g/3.8 oz of rye flour
50g/1.7 oz of brown sugar
80g/2.8 oz of flour
1 teaspoon of baking powder
2 tablespoons of milk
half a teaspoon of salt

Mix the butter and sugar to make a paste.

Mix the flour, rye flour, baking powder and salt. Add
them to the butter mix and milk and stir. Make a dough.

Wrap the dough in plastic wrap/clingfilm and place in the
refrigerator for 1 and a half hours.

Roll out the dough. cut into biscuit/cookie shapes. Place
on a baking sheet and cook in a preheated oven at
190C/375f for 10 minutes.

Serve topped with cream cheese and lingonberry jam.

Sand Cake

Ingredients

dough

700g/1 and a half lb of flour
1 teaspoon of baking powder
1 tablespoon of orange zest
200ml/6.6 fl oz of orange juice
210g/7.4 oz oz of butter
280g/10 oz of sugar
2 beaten eggs
170ml.5.5 fl oz of milk

filling

680ml/1 and a half pint of milk
400g/14 oz of butter
120g/4.2 oz of plum jam
180g/6.3 oz of cornflour/cornstarch
80g/2.8 oz of sugar
2 drops of vanilla essence

For the dough, mix the flour, baking powder, sugar and butter. Add the zest and juice. Add the beaten egg and milk and make a dough.

Cut the dough into six bits. Roll out one piece of dough so it is about 25 cm x 33 cm/10 in x 13 in.

Put on a baking sheet and cook in a preheated oven at 180C/350F for 15 minutes. Cut the edges to make a circle shape. Keep the off cuts. Repeat this process with the other pieces of dough.

With the off cuts of pastry, crush into breadcrumbs.

For the filling put the cornstarch, sugar, vanilla essence and milk in a pan. Bring to the boil then cook on a low heat for5 minus- until thickened. Cool. Add the butter to the mix.

Put a pastry piece on a plate. spread over some jam Put another pieces of pastry on top. Spread with the other mix. Repeat the process for the rest of the pastry. Finish with the milk mix over the top of the cake. Sprinkle the breadcrumbs on top.

Estonian Christmas Facts

The shortest day in Estonia is the Winter Solstice on the 21st December. The day is 6 hours long.

Since Estonia's independence from the Soviet Union in 1991 Christmas has been an official holiday again and many modern Estonian Christmas traditions have been based on those of the Scandinavian countries.

Estonia has a lot of forests and therefore a lot of real Christmas trees.

Christmas trees can be bought from of the state forests and paid for via a mobile phone app.

The traditional Estonian Christmas dinner is:

pork with sauerkraut
blood sausage
pork in jelly (Sült)

Side dishes include:

lingonberry jam,
roast potatoes
pickled pumpkins
potato salad
pickled cucumbers
rye bread

Baked Apples

Ingredients

4 cored apples – only create one hole in the apple
60g/2.11 oz of brown sugar
50g/1.7 oz of butter
1 teaspoon of cinnamon
150ml/5 fl oz of water.

Mix the brown sugar, cinnamon and butter. Stuff the apples with the mix.

Put the apples in a baking dish. Pour in the water. Cook in a preheated oven at 190C/375F for 1 hour 10 minutes.

Oatmeal Cookies

Ingredients

180g/6.3 oz of oatmeal
30g/1 oz of raisins
75g/2.6 oz of flour
75g/2.6 oz of sugar
1 teaspoon of baking powder
60g/2.11 oz of honey
1 egg
drop of vanilla essence
60g/2.11 oz of melted butter

Mix the flour, oatmeal, sugar, salt and baking powder. Add the honey, vanilla, egg and melted butter and mix to make a dough. Add the raisins. Mix, then cover the bowl and leave for 40 minutes.

Roll the dough into balls. Put on a baking tray lined with parchment paper. Press the cookies down a little. Cook in a preheated oven at 180C/350F for 25 minutes.

Curd Cheese and Berries

Ingredients

300g/10 oz of curd cheese
berries
300ml/10 fl oz of whipping cream
1 teaspoon of vanilla extract
4 teaspoons of sugar

Push the cheese through a sieve.

Mix the sugar and cream. Whisk to make a stiff mix. Add the cheese and vanilla and mix. Top with berries. Put into glasses. Top with berries.

Chill for 30 minutes.

Kringle

Ingredients

300g/10 oz of flour
1 tablespoon of sugar
3 and a half teaspoon of yeast
half a teaspoon of salt
200ml/6.5 fl oz of milk
35g/1.2 oz of butter
1 egg yolk

filling

55g/2 oz of butter
70g/2.5 oz of sugar
2 teaspoons of cinnamon

Mix the yeast and sugar in a bowl. Warm the milk a little and stir in. Melt the butter and add with the egg yolk.

Mix the flour and salt. add the milk mix and make a dough. Form into a ball. coat a bowl with some oil. Put the dough in it, then cover the bowl with clingfilm/plastic wrap. Leave for 1 hour in a warm place.

Mix the filling ingredients - butter, sugar and cinnamon.

Roll out the dough to make a rectangle shape. Spread the most of the filling on top. Roll up the dough. Cut almost to one end on the long side of the roll. Braid the two pieces. Brush with the rest of the filling.

Place on a baking sheet lined with parchment paper and

cook in a preheated oven at 200C/400F for 25 minutes.

Carrot Pie

Ingredients

dough

30g/1 oz of yeast
1 egg
110g/4 oz of butter
270g/9.5 oz of flour
80ml/3 fl oz of warm milk
1 tablespoon of sugar
salt
half a teaspoon of crushed cardamon
egg for glaze

filling

520g/1.1 lb of grated carrots
1 teaspoon of sugar
2 grated boiled eggs
55g/2 oz of butter
pinch of nutmeg
pinch of salt

Put milk in a bowl with the yeast and leave for 3 minutes.

Put the yeast, flour, cardamom, sugar, butter, egg and
some salt in a bowl. Make a dough. Knead for 5 minutes.
Grease a bowl with some oil. Make a ball from the dough
and put it in the dough. Cover with clingfilm/plastic wrap
and leave for an hour in a warm place.

for the filling, put the carrots in a pan with a little water.
Cook for 7 minutes. Add the rest of the filling ingredients.

Roll out the dough into a rectangular shape. Spread the
filling on top. Roll up the dough. Brush some beaten egg
on top. Cook in a preheated oven at 180C/356F for 30
minutes- until browned.

Gingerbread

Pipparkogid

Ingredients

460g/2 cups of sugar
1 teaspoon of baking soda
a pinch of nutmeg
1 teaspoon of crushed clove
3 teaspoons of cinnamon
half a teaspoon of crushed cardamon
1 tablespoon of grated orange peel
230g/8 oz of butter
800g/6 and half cups of flour
350ml of hot water

icing

1 teaspoon of lemon juice
100g/3.5 oz of icing/confectioners' sugar
half an egg white

Put 150g/5.3 oz of sugar in a pan. cook on a low heat until the sugar has formed a brown liquid. Pour half the hot water into the pan and mix. add the rest of the sugar and water and stir. Add the clove, nutmeg, cinnamon, cardamon and nutmeg and mix. Add the orange peel. Add the butter and stir in. Leave to cool. Add the flour and baking soda and mix to make a dough. Wrap in clingfilm/plastic wrap and place in the refrigerator for 4 days.

Roll the dough out. Cut into the shape of your choice - e.g. tree shapes.

Place on a baking sheet lined with parchment paper and cook in a preheated oven at 200C/392F for 10 minutes.

Whisk the icing ingredients together. Ice the gingerbread when they have cooled.

Cranberry Pudding

Ingredients

250ml/1 cup of cranberry juice
180g/6.3 oz of semolina
60g/2 oz of sugar
cold milk
berries
750ml/3 cups of water

Mix the cranberry juice, sugar and water together. Put in
a pan and bring to the boil. Add the semolina, stir well,
then cook on a low heat for 15 minutes.

Cool, then whisk into a foam.

Add berries when serving.

Barley Bread

Ingredients

1 grated carrot
480ml/2 cups of sour cream
1 egg
120ml/half a cup of melted butter
70g/half a cup of wholemeal flour
150g/5.3 oz of barley flour
1 teaspoon of baking soda
1 teaspoon of salt
4 tablespoons of sugar
butter

Cook the carrot in some butter in a pan for 5 minutes.

Mix the barley and wholemeal flour and the baking soda.

Mix the egg, sugar, salt and sour cream in a bowl. Add to the flour and mix. Add the carrot and melted butter and mix well.

Pour the mix into a baking dish. Cook in a preheated oven at 176C/350F for 40 minutes.

Rye Bread Cake

Ingredients

130g/4.5 oz of rye bread
110g/4 oz of ground hazelnuts
lingonberry jam
chopped chocolate
3 tablespoons of cocoa powder
1 teaspoon of baking powder
4 egg whites
4 egg yolks
140g/5 oz of brown sugar
whipped cream

Put the bread in a blender and blend to create breadcrumbs.

Mix the breadcrumbs, hazelnuts, baking powder and cocoa powder.

Whisk the egg yolk and sugar to make a thick mix. Add the breadcrumb mix.

Whisk the egg whites until stiff. Add to the breadcrumb mix.

Put the mix into two greased cake tins. Cook in a preheated oven at 180C/350F for 20 minutes. Leave to cool.

Spread cream on the top of one of the cakes. Spread over some lingonberry jam. Put the other cake on top. Spread cream on top. Sprinkle chopped chocolate on top.

Curd Cheesecake

Ingredients

base

1 egg
80g/2.8 oz of butter
80g/2.8 oz of sugar
220g/7.7 oz of flour
2 teaspoons of baking powder

filling

230g/8.11 oz of mandarin segments
230g/8.11 oz of sour cream
550g/1.2 lb of curd cheese
130g/4.5 oz of melted butter
2 eggs
2 and a half tablespoons of cornflour/cornstarch
3 teaspoons of vanilla sugar
235g/8 oz of sugar
220g/7.7 oz of whipping cream
1 tablespoon of lemon zest
For the base mix all the ingredients and make a dough.
Line a round cake tin with the dough.

For the filling mix the butter, cornstarch, sugar, vanilla
sugar and eggs. Mix well to make a batter.

Add the whipping cream, curd cheese, lemon zest and
sour cream and mix. Pour half the mix into the cake tin.

Put the mandarin segments on top. Add the rest of the filling.

Cook in a preheated oven at 160C/320F for 1 hour.

Semla

Ingredients

340g/12 oz of flour
1 teaspoon of yeast
3 tablespoons of sugar
1 beaten egg
half a teaspoon of cardamom
60ml/2 fl oz of warm milk
40g/1.4 oz of melted butter
4 tablespoons of warm water

paste

25g/1 quarter of a cup of ground almonds
50g/half a cup of confectioners' icing sugar
1 egg white

whipped cream
egg yolk for glaze
confections'/icing sugar

Put the warm water, yeast and a pinch of sugar in a bowl.
Leave for 6 minutes.

Mix the milk, beaten egg and butter together. Add to the
bowl. Add the flour, sugar, salt and cardamom. Mix and
knead to make a dough.

Put the dough in an oiled bowl. Cover the bowl with
plastic wrap/clingfilm and leave for 1 hour to double in
size.

Make 12 balls from the dough. Put on a greased baking
tray. Leave for 35 minutes t double in size. Brush with
some beaten egg. Cook in a preheated oven at 175C/350F
for 25 minutes.

For the almond paste, whip the egg white until stiff.
Gently add the sugar and almonds.

Cool the buns. Cut the buns in half. Spread on some
almond paste. Add some whipped cream. Put the top back
on the buns.

Dust with confectioners' sugar.

Milk Soup

Ingredients

600ml/2 and a half cups of water
110g/4 oz of barley
800ml/3 and a half cups of milk
1 teaspoon of sugar
1 tablespoon of butter
dill

Put the water in a pan and bring to the boil. Add the barley and salt then cook on a low heat for 25 minutes.

Add the milk and cook for 5 minutes - until the barley is cooked. Add butter.

Top with some fresh dill.

Cranberry Kissel

Ingredients

240g/8 oz of cranberries
1.2 litres/5 cups of water
240g/8 oz of sugar
60g/half a cup of potato flour
110ml/3.7 fl oz of cold water

Boil the water. Add the cranberries. Boil for 6 minutes.

Drain and keep the liquid. Rub the cranberries through a
sieve. Put the liquid and cranberries back in the pan Add
the sugar and cook on a low heat for 7 minutes.

Mix the potato flour and cold water. Remove the pan
from the heat and add the potato flour mix to the pan.
Stir well.

Cook the mix on a low heat for 7 minutes.

Serve cool.

Mulled Wine

Glögi

Ingredients

700ml/3 cups of red wine
90ml/3 fl oz of rum or vodka
7 cloves
8 tablespoons of almonds
8 tablespoons of raisins
2 pieces of sliced ginger
200ml/7 fl oz of orange juice
100ml/3.3 fl oz of lemon juice
1 tablespoon of lemon zest
1 tablespoon of orange zest
1 tablespoon of brown sugar
1 teaspoon of nutmeg
2 cardamon pods
1 stock of cinnamon

Put the wine, lemon juice and orange juice in a pan. Mix, then add the cardamon, cloves, ginger, sugar and nutmeg. Cook on a moderate heat for 12 minutes. Do not boil as the alcohol is needed/

Put raisins and almonds in cups. Put the mulled wine in the cups.